HOW TO CARE FOR YOUR RABBIT

The Complete Guide from Kit to Adult

By RabbitCare Specialists

Table of Contents

Introduction

In this book, you'll find everything you need to know about how to properly care for, train, feed, vaccinate and raise your kit (Baby rabbit, also known as kittens) into the perfect little hopping ball of fur. It is the essential guide which covers everything you need to know. From advice on feeding, training and keeping them entertained, to staying on top of their vaccinations and correcting bad behaviors. It is our job to help you understand your kit and help you give him or her the best home you can provide. The decision to adopt your first kitten or rabbit is a monumental one for both you and for the rabbit. He will be one of the family. Whether you are thinking about getting a rabbit or you have adopted or bought one and you want to know how to best take care of it, or even if you have adopted or bought one and are starting to panic about what you should be doing, then this book has been designed for you to make your relationship with this special kitten or rabbit a lasting one.

We will cover everything you need to know throughout the rabbit's life cycle and talk about things such as behavioral problems in rabbits, such as avoiding the litter box, spraying, excessive grunting and other attention-seeking or destructive behaviors. These types of behaviors are easier to stop early on but even if you have adopted an older rabbit it can be corrected by identifying the problem, then initiating a program of gradual retraining. Remember that there are no bad rabbits, only uninformed owners.

You can keep this book as a guide or user manual throughout your rabbit's life as it covers all the areas you need to know so keep it handy on the book shelf. We believe that rabbits make for great pets and can be easier to maintain than some other common pets such as dogs which require more upkeep. It's exciting having a pet and we hope through this book that you can give your rabbit the love and care that all animals deserve.

Bringing Your Kit Home

Owning a new rabbit will certainly bring much joy into your life. Rabbits are naturally shy, timid animals but through socializing they can be affectionate and loving animals. When you first get your rabbit, let them settle in for the first 24 hours and try not to stress them or disturb them too much as they are timid and will find the new environment and change in scenery a little unsettling at first. They will be very nervous and frightened at first and will need this time to adapt to their new surroundings, such as getting used to the sights , smells, and sounds of their new home. After the first 24 hours, continue to be gentle with them but begin trying to handle more frequently over the next few weeks to get them used to being handled and being around people so they get accustomed to people's company and to help socialize them. I don't think this will be hard to do as you will probably want to cuddle them a lot anyway as they are cute, adorable little critters. Supply them with fresh hay and bedding and comfortable new bed which is dry and quiet. If they are over the age of four months, they should have some water and vegetables.

Give them plenty of reassurance, time and affection and let them adjust to new surroundings before making introductions to other animals or people in the household. Ensure that all doors and windows are closed and a guard is in front of the fireplace if you have one. The kits are small and agile and will like to explore every area of the house. For kits older than a month, make sure they know where the bed, litter box and food and water bowls are, this is important and should be done early.

For quieter dogs or pets used to rabbits or other animals, introductions can be made using a strong rabbit carrier on the second day. Keep the dog on a lead initially, placing the carrier on a high surface and allowing controlled introductions short and frequently. Most dogs soon calm down when they realize the newcomer is not particularly interesting and you can progress to direct meetings with the dog, on a lead initially for safety. Do not leave the new pet alone with dogs or other rabbits until your kit is well established in the household and introductions have been made numerous times. If you don't have the pen or carrier then carry the kitten gently and make sure to be ready to pull the kitten away if the dog get too excited as they may get carried away and playfully lick or nibble the kitten. Slow, calm, patient and frequent introductions is the key.

Socialization is important for your kit to live confidently and safely in your household. A kit raised in a home or adoption center where staff are aware of the importance of socialization should cope well with the move to a new family. However, litters born and raised outdoors, or in some shelters that have remained isolated or kits from wild rabbit litters, may not have enough experience with humans to adapt fully to a family or may take vastly longer to adjust so be patient.

Bottle Milk and Nutrition for Kits

Sometimes it can be scary if the mother stops feeding her litter or if it is up to you to milk the kits. You just need to follow some simple procedures and as time goes on you will get used to feeding them. If you're responsible for taking care of kittens in the first few months of their lives you need to know what milk to use and how often to feed them. Baby rabbits should be fed Kitten Milk Replacer (KMR) or goat milk, which you can buy at pet stores or sometimes at your vets. Kittens will drink milk from weeks zero to week four, then they will slowly transition from milk to pellets and hay at around four to five weeks. This process of moving them to solid food is known as weaning, which we will cover in the next chapter. Kits that are still with their mother are easier to take care of as the mother will milk them until she cannot produce any more milk and then she will naturally and gradually stop them from breast feeding and offer them other sources of food, which in the wild would be weeds, grasses, wildflowers and vegetable plants or in the winter in would be twigs, buds, bark, conifer needles and any remaining green plants. For domesticated rabbits they will transition to pellets, vegetables and hay.

What are the kit's milk requirements for the first four weeks?

• If you own the newborn kitten and its mother is there you should have nothing to worry about when it comes to feeding them. Their mother's milk provides 100 percent of the nutritional needs and you don't have to give them milk until after the first four weeks of life where you can start introducing pellets and hay

• If the mother rabbit becomes sick, cannot produce enough milk, or the kittens are found as orphans, you may use a milk replacement and feed them with syringes or eyedroppers

• When feeding the kit for the first time, up to two weeks, hold the syringe or teat close to the kitten's mouth and she will instinctively start feeding.

• When feeding, make sure you loosely cover the bunny in a soft face cloth or hand towel and lay it on your lap or in the crook of your arm. If it will NOT eat this way you can improvise and try setting them somewhere safe and comfortable. It is ABSOLUTELY CRUCIAL to let the baby eat at it's own pace, especially if it is not suckling from the syringe willingly. If you squirt the liquid too quickly you can aspirate (get liquid in) the lungs and the rabbit will suffocate. So be patient with them and let them feed at their own pace.

• Formulated milk and bottles can be bought from pet stores, vets or online and they all have information on how to use them and what ages of the kitten they are suitable for. Milk replacement or formulated milk comes in tubs or drums and is a dry powder or liquid. Follow the instructions on the packet on how many scoops to use and how much water to mix if needed. The amount of milk to feed the kitten per day should be on the instructions of the formulated milk. As a rough guide you can use this:

Rabbits 0 – 1 week old: 4 – 5 cc formula.

Rabbits 1 - 2 weeks old: 10 – 15 cc formula.

Rabbits 2 – 3 weeks old: 15 – 30 cc formula.

Rabbits 3 – 6 weeks old or until they are weaned get 30 cc formula.

Weaning Your Kits

What Is Weaning?

Weaning is the process of transitioning kittens from mother's milk/formulated milk to solid food. During weaning the kits gradually progress from dependence on a mother's care to social independence. Think of it as the early teenage years of the kitten world minus the pimples. The kits will start to gain their independence and want to take on the world by themselves and their behaviors and personalities will start to become more apparent. Ideally, weaning is handled entirely by the mother rabbit (fun fact: a female rabbit is called a doe and a male rabbit is called a buck). If the kits in your care have been separated from their mother or if you are fostering a litter or you have a pregnant Doe about to give birth and you are seeing the young ones through to a successful weaning process, then this information will be important. Hand rearing of rabbits is rarely successful if you are inexperienced and not very common. You will usually get them from a pet store already weaned. For those who do need information on this, you can read on.

What Age Should Kittens Be Weaned?

Rabbits in the wild wean their litters at 4 weeks of age or earlier. This is because they are already very pregnant with their next litter and they simply abandon the 4-week-old kits in order to go off and dig themselves a new burrow. The gestation or pregnancy period for rabbits is around 28-32 days. Crazy, huh!? Now you know why they have the expression, "breeding like rabbits" and why you should make sure your rabbit gets spade, especially if you are planning to own a few rabbits.

The weaning process for domesticated rabbits normally begins when kittens are around four weeks old and is usually completed when they reach six to eight weeks. If you oversee weaning an orphaned kitten please remember that weaning should not be attempted at too early of an age. Generally, when a kitten's eyes are open and able to focus and he/she is steady on their feet, the introduction of pellets, vegetables or hay can safely begin which is usually around four to five weeks.

How Long Does It Take to Wean a Kitten (Baby Rabbit)?

The process typically takes between four and six weeks with most kittens completely weaned by the time they're eight to ten weeks old.

How Do I Start the Weaning Process?

It's important to remember that abrupt removal from the mother rabbit (doe) can have a negative effect on the kittens' health and socialization skills. They learn to eat, use a litter box and play, among other things, by observing their mother. Whenever possible, kittens should remain with their mother during the weaning process, as she will inherently know what to do.

When the kits reach four weeks old, you can place the doe in a separate area for a few hours at a time to reduce their dependency on mother's milk and her overall presence. Keep them in their own specific area such as their cage or box that they have already been staying to keep the environment familiar. Place a litter box, food bowl and water bowl in the cage or area with them and give them about 60 percent of the recommended commercial feed ration on the first day of weaning, 80 percent the following day and the full amount on the third day. There is special baby rabbit food you can get from pet stores and make hay available all at times during this period, but replace the hay daily to stop enterotoxaemia. As the kittens become more independent, they can spend more time away from their mother until they are completely weaned.

Newly weaned rabbits are at risk of suffering from enteritis or gastrointestinal tract infection. It's important to keep an eye on your kits' fecal output once they're weaned. Feeding too many carbohydrates and too little fiber can lead to this problem for rabbits of 1 to 2 months of age. Enteritis usually presents itself in the form of diarrhea. Your vet might be able to save your kit by prescribing antibiotics and recommending dietary changes but consult a vet if your kits have diarrhea as this can be fetal for young rabbits at an early age.

Beyond the Litter Box

Yes, you can litter train your little fall of fur, but spaying or neutering should be done first if it hasn't been done already as it is almost impossible to litter train them without it. Females are neutered around 4 - 6 months old and males around 3 – 4 months old. If you can't wait for them to roam about the house before this, be prepared to have clean up the mess. It is harder to train them if they get into the habit of using your room as one large litter box. Rabbits like to have enough room to stretch out in their boxes so if you have more than one rabbit you have to allow enough room for both of them, so if it is a box or cage, then make sure there is room for them both. Just like cats, bunnies can easily be litter trained, which is specifically why so many bunny owners are able to merely let their bunnies run free within the house. Most rabbits prefer to carry out their business in one spot, thus litter training comes naturally, but it is recommended to get medium to large litter trays.

Most rabbits can be litter-trained and allowed supervised freedom in the house. Start with a large cat litter box; put newspaper and/or rabbit-safe litter on the bottom and cover it with lots of fresh oat hay. Since a rabbit usually urinates in one corner of his space, this is where you place the litter box. Once the bunny uses the box reliably, you can let him out into a larger area, putting out a second box. Keep the rabbit confined to a small space until they are very good with his box.

Do use:

• Newspapers, Crown Bedding (or similar) recycled newspaper pellet litter/animal bedding
• Carefresh (or similar) paper pulp litter/animal bedding
• Wood stove pellets (these are used as fuel for woodstoves, but are actually great as bunny litter pellets)
• Ground corncob pet litter/bedding
• Always check the label. Don't buy litter that cedar, cedar oils, zinc or the clumping clay

Do **NOT** use:

- No clay litter! This can cause serious respiratory problems
- No Cat Works litter! This can cause zinc poisoning and can be fatal
- No Pine or Cedar litters! These can also be fatal

Signs of a House-Soiling problem would include the following:

- A consistent pattern of urinating and/or rabbit droppings outside the litter box
- Urine spraying which would be urine marks around doorways or new objects in the house
- Spending longer than a normal amount of time in the litter box
- Going to the litter box more often than normal

Potential causes of House-Soiling:

- A dirty litter box or inadequate number of litter boxes in the home. There should be at least one box per rabbit but an extra one is recommended, especially in bigger houses. If you have multiple boxes the litter boxes need to be in various locations in the house, not all in one room.
- Litter box is in a remote, noisy or unpleasant surrounding
- Litter box is inappropriate. Covered boxes can maintain odors and large rabbits may not be able to move around enough in small boxes

- Wrong type of litter or sudden change in litter type
- Infrequent changing of litter box
- Infrequent routines or travelling a lot
- Having multiple rabbits

Here are a few other tips for those stubborn, "outside-the-box" bunnies:

If perhaps accidents occur, mop up urine with a paper towel and pick up stray poop and place both in the litter box. This will help get the message across that the litter box is the place that they should do their business. You need to understand that rabbits take a while to get used to their litter box. Sometimes they leave a few droppings next to the box, or they urinate over the edge of their box. This is normal, so placing a plastic mat under their litter box or putting the litter box on a tile floor makes it easier to clean up these little mistakes.

If your bunny is inconsistent on going in one corner of the room, sometimes it's easier to give in to their stubbornness and place a litter box in that corner. Sometimes when rabbits consistently choose another place to go they are trying to tell you that's where they want to go.

If your rabbit is pooping and spraying urine everywhere, this is a sign that your rabbit marking their territory. Both male and female rabbits do this, but this can go away if they are spayed/neutered in order to ease territorial feelings. Sometimes rabbits deliberately pee on your couch or bed because they're showing you who's Top Bunny in the house. You should correct their behavior immediately and show them who the real boss of the house is.

Be patient and persistent. Litter training takes time, especially if your rabbit has learned bad habits, it can take a while to retrain them as mentioned before. If you can see they're about to go outside their litter box (they may lift their tail or shimmy down in a seated position right before they go), try to pick them up and put them in the litter box.

In the event that you experience house-soiling then consider adjusting focused on some of the factors mentioned earlier. If the problem continues over a prolonged period of time, consult your veterinarian to investigate possible health issues. Please note that not all rabbits like litter box covers or liners. Make sure the litter box is in an easy-to-find, quiet place away from high-traffic areas of the house where other pets or people won't likely disrupt your rabbit's routine. Somewhere quiet and peaceful where he will not be disturbed.

Rabbit Vaccinations

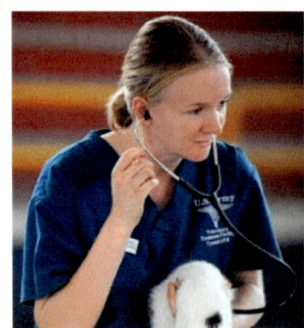

Routine vaccination has greatly reduced the extent of several rabbit diseases (including some that can prove fatal). It is vital that your rabbit has all the necessary vaccinations and boosters. Please consult your local vet for more information on vaccinations.

What vaccines does my rabbit need?

Anytime after 6 weeks of age you should have your rabbit vaccinated against myxomatosis. Myxomatosis is a terrible disease which is almost always fatal and can cause the rabbit to suffer leading up this. Rabbits need vaccinations to prevent/protect against many diseases, especially the two major and most common rabbit diseases which are myxomatosis and rabbit (Viral) Haemorrhagic Disease (R(V)HD) which causes intense suffering to rabbits. Combined vaccines provided by your vet offers protection against both diseases and rabbits should be vaccinated at around five weeks.

• Myxomatosis

What is it?

This virus is spread by mites, fleas and mosquitoes. Myxomatosis is widespread in British wild rabbits. Its early symptoms include puffy swellings around face, the eyes (which can cause blindness), the ears and around the anus or genitals. High fever follows then eating and drinking gradually becomes very difficult. Death occurs within 10-14 days.

How is it spread?

• Contact with other rabbits carrying or infected with the virus.
• Insects carrying the disease (mainly from biting insects)
• Environment (dirty/infected litter boxes, unclean environment)

- There is no treatment for this and recovery is rare meaning they may have to be put down
- Rabbits already vaccinated can catch milder forms, often recovering with intensive veterinary care.

• Rabbit (Viral) Haemorrhagic Disease (R(V)HD)

What is it?

The rabbit Viral Hemorrhagic Disease is a highly contagious disease which is caused by a Calicivirus that affects only rabbits of the *Oryctolagus_cuniculus* species. This includes both wild and domesticated European rabbits, from which our own domesticated rabbits descended from. It has not been known to affect and North American native rabbits or hares. Rabbits may die within 48 hours of exposure to this virus and the death rate of rabbits exposed to this virus is very high, between 50% and 100%.

Symptoms:

- High fever
- Loss of appetite
- Lethargy

- Blue mucous membranes
- Seizures
- Coma
- Respiratory difficulty
- Sudden death

How is it spread?

- Humans (from humans that have been in contact with infected rabbits or with objects contaminated by the virus.)
- Feces from an infected rabbit.
- Direct contact with infected rabbit.
- Contact of rabbit with inanimate objects contaminated by the virus.
- Contact with rabbit products such as wool, fur, meat from infected rabbit.

Protection:

- Maintain good personal hygiene.
- Wash your hands prior to handling your pet.
- Control insects such as flies.
- If you encounter other rabbits, disinfect your clothing.
- Provide regular flea treatment to reduce the chance of infection spread from parasites.
- When you are introducing new rabbit, place the rabbit in quarantine for 5 days before allowing contact with other rabbits.

Your Rabbit's First Month at Home

If you have just bought or adopted an adult rabbit, moved to a new house or even just borrowed your friends rabbit while they are on holiday, then your rabbit will likely take a few days to settle into the unfamiliar environment. If it's the former, you can start thinking about long-term care and making sure you're prepared for a long, happy life together. Here are some basics to get you started in the first month.

Bedding: You need to get the right kind of bed for your rabbit to sleep in. Creating the right conditions for your new rabbit is important. Make sure bedding is soft and washable, and place it inside a basket, small box, cage, cozy corner or a particularly ideal quiet and sunny spot of the house.

Travelling or transporting: Keeping your rabbit safe when travelling to your new home. rabbit carriers are the safest, most comfortable way to travel. Before hitting the road, take time to familiarize your rabbit with the carrier by storing toys in it or making it a cozy place for a nap. Good toys for rabbits are easy to find and widely available at pet stores so make sure he/she has some favorite toys and try and if you are just picking up your new rabbit, get him used to the toys if possible before putting them in the carrier.

Rabbit Proofing: Rabbits have a habit of chewing things like cords and tubes. Make sure you remove books from the bottom shelves and make sure wires and cords are out of the way and hidden. Keep plants of the ground unless you want them nibbled at. Have some toys to keep them distracted or when they try and nibble things they shouldn't, refamiliarize them with the toy and give them a treat when they play with it. You can get toys at the pet store or try some of these homemade ideas:

- Toilet paper and paper towel rolls
- Newspaper and white scrap paper (ink isn't harmful, just gives dirty feet)
- Straw baskets

- Canning jar rings
- Rolled oats box stuffed with hay
- Soft drink can with pebble inside for noise
- Wire ball with bell inside (sold in stores as a cat or bird toy)
- Cardboard boxes (tape shut then cut small doors)
- Old towels to push around and dig at

Manicure for Rabbits

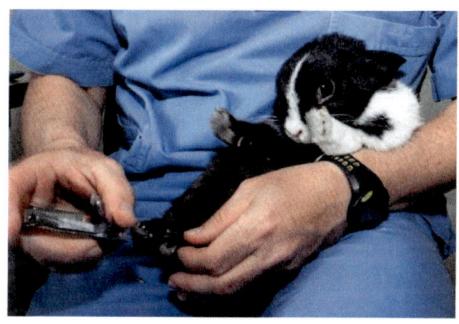

Calm, enjoyable nail-trimming sessions are not only possible but may be necessary. Pet rabbits cannot dig or wear down their claws to their nails may grow long and need trimmed. Check out the following tips for getting rabbits to relax while you trim them, turning nail-clipping sessions into enjoyable human-rabbit together time. Nail trimming is a necessary part of grooming your pet rabbit as their nails continuously grow (just like their teeth) so if they are not naturally wearing them down outside they will need to be trimmed using nail clippers. If you have never trimmed your rabbit's nails and you do not have someone to help you, you may want to seek help from a pet groomer or veterinary staff or take them to the vet or groomer to get this done. If you have a young rabbit, make sure you take the opportunity to start trimming their nails while they are young and on a regular basis so they can get used to it.

How to Trim Rabbit Nails

First, gather the supplies that you will need as well as a friend to hold your rabbit for you. You don't want to have to start and stop once you have your rabbit ready so get everything together in one place. Get yourself a good pair of nail clippers made for cats or rabbits, a towel, styptic powder opened up (to be ready in case you clip a nail too short) and treats for your rabbit.

Have the holder wrap your rabbit in a towel or blanket to help keep them calm and safely restrained. A rabbit can kick and hurt their back so make sure you are handling them correctly and supporting them well. If they start to struggle, stop the process. Set your rabbit back down, and try again once your rabbit calms down. You can use treats to reward your rabbit and get them used to being held in the towel or blanket.

Once your rabbit is wrapped in the towel and is calm, trim only the tip of the nails. Place the clippers on the nail where the cut is to be made. Slowly squeeze the trimmers to cut the nail and if the rabbit flinches, move a bit toward the tip of the nail (you may be too close to the quick). Make the cut in a firm, swift motion to avoid the risk of crushing the nail.

If a nail is accidentally cut too short, don't panic and remain calm. Pack some of the styptic powder on the end of the nail to stop the bleeding. Unless the nail has been cut too short, there is no reason for alarm if you accidentally cut a quick. Everyone who regularly cuts nails on their pet has trimmed one too short at some point in time so do not feel too bad about it and try again.

Note: Make sure you give your Rabbit a treat after the whole process to reward them.

What not to Do?

• If your rabbit resists, don't raise your voice or punish her.
• Never attempt a clipping when your rabbit is agitated or you're upset. And don't rush, you may cut into the quick.
• Don't try to trim all your rabbit's claws at one time if you feel they are getting agitated.
• Do NOT de-claw. This surgery involves amputating the end of a rabbit's toes and is highly discouraged. Instead, trim regularly, provide your rabbit with appropriate scratching posts and ask your veterinarian about soft plastic covers for your rabbit's claws.

Overweight Rabbits

Obesity is a widespread problem in pets and, as with humans, can be detrimental to the health of a rabbit. The overweight pet has many added stresses upon his body and is at an increased risk of diabetes, liver problems and joint pain. Obesity develops when energy intake exceeds energy requirements. The excess energy is then stored as fat. Once a pet is obese, he may remain obese even after excessive caloric intake stops. Most cases of obesity are related to simple overfeeding coupled with lack of exercise and can be a problem with house rabbits.

Once the rabbit becomes an adult, at about six months, having fresh water and hay should be available at all times and a handful of fresh vegetables daily. Senior rabbits, age a year and above, should maintain the same feeding regimen. Obesity is less common in rabbits than in dogs. As a subjective assessment of body condition, you should be able to feel the backbone and palpate the ribs in an animal of healthy weight. If you cannot feel your pet's ribs without pressing, there is too much fat.

We recommend that you consult your pet's vet before starting on a weight loss program, but here are some tips for dieting which should include these major areas:

• Correct Diet. Overweight animals consume more calories than they require. Work with your veterinarian to determine your pet's caloric requirements, select a suitable food and calculate how much to feed. The diet should contain a normal level of a moderately fermentable fiber and the type of fat that prevents the skin and coat from deteriorating during weight loss. Diets that dilute calories with high fiber lead to increased stool volumes, frequent urges to defecate and variable decreases in nutrient digestibility.

• Exercise. Increasing physical activity can be a valuable contributor to both weight loss and maintenance. Regular exercise burns more calories, reduces appetite, changes body composition and will increase your pet's resting metabolic rate. If you keep them to a confined space, let them out to roam more often or consider getting a bigger living area for them.

• Owner Behavior Modification. A successful weight management program requires permanent changes in the behaviors that have allowed the pet to become overweight. Perhaps you are giving your pet too many treats, for example, or not giving him enough opportunities to exercise.

If you are committed to your pet's weight loss, here are some important things you can do:

• Feed your pet several small meals throughout the day.
• Feed all meals and treats in the pet's bowl only.
• Reduce snacks or treats.
• Provide non-food related attention instead of treats.

Keeping Your Rabbit Happy at Home

You may not think of rabbits as paying much attention when their owners come and go, but some rabbits can develop separation anxiety when they form a particularly strong bond with their owners. So just as you love and miss the little ball of fur when you leave your rabbit for work or holiday, it is good to know that your rabbit misses you too. Keep an eye on your rabbits for signs of anxiety and take steps to ensure peace of mind in your absence. You have the privilege of taking your phone out and browsing your photos or screen saver of your bunny, but to my knowledge they don't have mobile phones for rabbits yet so they don't share the same privilege of looking at their favorite human companion when you leave, so be aware of rabbit separation anxiety.

Know the signs of separation anxiety. They can range from reclusiveness such as hiding in the hutch or bed to loss of appetite and not eating correctly. Basically, you're looking for anything that's different from their otherwise normal behavior. Make sure your rabbit's needs are being met. Rabbits are sensitive to routines and don't fall behind on litter box scooping and exercising them, despite demands on your schedule.

Provide opportunities for stimulation. Make sure your rabbits have plenty of engaging toys to enjoy while you're away and make the most of playtime when you're available. Playtime limits frustration and helps your rabbits maintain emotional balance. Check online for tips and pointers on more healthy ways to have fun with your rabbits or ask your veterinarian to help for ways to cope with separation anxiety issues. If you're still suffering from associated problems and don't see results, your veterinarian may need to take a closer look to rule out underlying health issues or provide additional treatment for anxiety.

Tips for keeping fuzzy wuzzy pants happy:

1)   Enough space and room. This applies to both his living area such as hutch or box and also to his roaming area for when

you let them out. This is especially important if you have more than one rabbit. They need double the space in their hutch and when they are let out so make sure there is ample room to do what they do best and hop around.

2)   Good diet. Rabbits have sensitive digestive systems that are always working as they feed constantly throughout the day. They need rabbit food, vegetables, hay and water. They like to graze on the hay which makes them happy so keep a fresh supply and change it daily.

3)   Company. Rabbits are sociable animals and they love company. Spend time with them and get them some friends. Guinea pigs make great companions and make sure if you get another rabbit that they are both neutered so you don't run into any unfortunate situations. Try giving them a little bath, rabbits actually enjoy a little water so fill up the bath tub with an inch of warm water and watch them play and groom themselves but not too much water as this might stress them, especially if they are not used to it.

4)   Neuter you rabbit. As well as stopping unfortunate situations, getting your rabbit neutered will make them easier to manage and make them more docile, friendly and affectionate.

5)   Entertainment. Rabbits like playing with toys so get yourself to the pet store and pick up some toys to play with and show them new environments to explore such as different rooms in the house or let them out in the garden if you have one.

Plenty of space to roam and explore also keeps them entertained.

6)   Vaccinate and health checks. Take them for regular health checks and vaccinate them to prevent or treat any health-related issues.

7)   Affection. Rabbits love affection and cuddles as much you love it too. Give them plenty of hugs and cuddles and let them know they are cared for.

8)   Digging. Rabbits naturally and instinctively love to dig as they are burrowing animals. Give them a place to dig such as a cardboard box with lots of newspapers or shredded papers and they will enjoy digging their way through it.

Managing Allergies to Rabbits

You may want to own a rabbit but you have allergies, are worried about allergies or you may already have a rabbit and find that your allergies are becoming a problem. The good news is that rabbits and people with allergies can live together! Phew! There's a lot you can do to make your life easier if you have allergies and a rabbit. Allergies to rabbits are caused by a reaction to certain proteins found primarily in secretions from a rabbit's skin and in a rabbit's saliva. These proteins stick to your rabbit's hair and skin and are released into the environment when shedding occurs. Another culprit of allergies could be the hay that you use, often Timothy hay can cause allergies to flare due to the dust it produces.

Some people report developing immunity or growing out of the allergy to their rabbit. While this is certainly possible, don't depend on it. It is also possible that the allergic reaction will get worse with more exposure. If you are getting a new rabbit and have concerns about allergies, consider a short-haired breed over a long-haired as they release less hair into your home environment. If you are interested in a purebred, consider a New Zealand White. These rabbits lack some of the layers of hair found on other breeds and so may produce less reaction. Keep in mind that all rabbits groom themselves and an allergic reaction is caused by saliva just as much as by hair.

Once you have a rabbit, diligence around the house is key to limiting allergies:

• Wipe down smooth surfaces in the home regularly and vacuum frequently as well
• Switch from timothy hay to another type of grass hay (orchard, bermuda, oat)
• Frequently wash and replace any bedding that your rabbit sleeps on
• You may want to restrict your rabbit's access to certain areas of the house. The allergic person's bedroom is a definite rabbit no-go zone
• Rooms with hardwood floors will retain less allergens and be easier to clean than carpet

- If you have only a few rooms in your house with carpet, you probably should keep your rabbit out of those

- Upholstered furniture pieces will retain a lot of allergens so you may choose to keep rabbits off them or out of rooms that contain them

- Providing the best rabbit care includes weekly brushing. It will be incredibly helpful in reducing allergic reactions because it helps prevent loose hair from getting into the air. Rabbits can shed every 3 months

- Cleaning the litter box regularly will also help because the proteins that cause a reaction in saliva, hair and dander are found in urine as well. Whenever possible, all grooming should be done by someone who isn't allergic to rabbits. It should also be done outdoors if possible

Products such as "AllerPet" and "AllerPet/C" are liquids/sprays which are applied regularly to fur and neutralize some of the fur allergens. Shampoo formulations are not recommended as some rabbits can stressed by baths with too much water. An inch of warm water is recommended and keep it out of their eyes and ears. The products mentioned work but can b expensive and should be used regularly if you decide to use them. An alternative is daily brushing (preferably outside) and wiping fur with a damp cloth. These products are not substitutes for previous recommendations.

You should also talk to your doctor about what anti-allergenic drugs you can take to make your life easier and other possible ways to manage the problem.

Rabbit Behavior Explained

Rabbits exhibit a wide range of emotions and behaviors so it is important to understand what it means and how to correct any bad behaviors. Behaviors can be anything from licking, binkying, growling, chewing, kicking up dirt, chinning or nose bonking. So what does it all mean?

Good and happy behavior:

Binkying. This is when your rabbit can jump, hop or leap, contorting and twisting their bodies and kicking their feet out. They are very expressive animals and this is a sign of joy and excitement. The fun ones are when they do a few binkies in succession creating an acrobatic display to behold.

The Bunny 500. This is when they zip around the room with bursts of speed, sometimes accompanied by binkies. They can sometimes do this when they know they are getting a treat. Like the binkies, they do this when they are excited and happy.

Flopping. When bunnies are content they can flop over roll about before settling down on their side. This is a happy, content bunny.

Licking. Bunnies show affection by licking as they would groom themselves. This means they are happy with you and grooming you, which they will also do to other rabbits or animals.

Purring or teeth grinding. Teeth grinding can often make you a little concerned when they grind their teeth but in most cases don't fret, it's nothing to worry about, it just means they are happy with you, usually when you are petting them and it is usually associated with the purring. If it is not associated with the petting, it happens frequently and is louder than when you pet them, or when they look distressed or hunched over, then it could be a sign of discomfort or pain. In those cases, it may be a health issue you need to get checked out.

Bad or aggressive behavior:

Growling. This is a sign of distress or anger. It could be territorial or their way of getting you to back off and give them space. It can be accompanied with aggressive behavior so just take caution in those situation.

Screaming. A sign of intense pain or can be associated to times close to death. Seek veterinarian assistance immediately if this happens.

Kicking up dirt. Not literally kicking up dirt, this term comes from in the wild, where it would be literal and it is their way of showing aggression to other animals or rabbits. For domesticated rabbits this will translate to kicking their feet up as they hop away from you. Sometimes happens after you do something that displeases them.

Chinning. A way of marking territory and claiming it. Rabbits have scent glands in their chins which is used for leaving their scent or mark.

Nose bonking or nudging. Used when exploring environments or objects by sniffing and nudging them. It could be their greeting at first but can also indicate attention seeking, telling you that you are in their way or that they want attention or petting.

Sometimes nudges can be followed by nips, just to really get your attention.

Digging. Another way to get attention, they might try and dig into your feet or legs. Give them a little cuddle and they should stop.

Nipping. As mentioned, nips are a way to get attention. They don't mean any harm but can be very annoying. Make loud noises or screams when they do this will discourage them and eventually they will stop doing it. Sometimes they can be a warning depending on the situation, such as territorial if you invade their space. Spaying or neutering can stop this behavior.

Thumping. Rabbits thump when they feel threatened or in danger. They thump their hind legs as a warning to others. This behavior is very common among free-roaming rabbits who want to inform others of a potential attack.

Rabbits have always been regarded as "the quiet pet" and it's true that they generally aren't well known for disturbing the neighbors. In most cases, rabbits communicate with people today using their body language and behavior as described above. Nonetheless, there's a list of sounds that you might have discovered rabbits make although most of them are made at quite a low level.

Happy Rabbit Sounds:

Clucking. Rabbit clucking doesn't resemble the clucking sounds of a chicken, it's also a lot quieter. However, a clucking sound coming from a rabbit means that they're satisfied with what they're nibbling on.

Purring. A lot like purring for a cat they both mean "happy and content". However, cats purr using their throat while rabbits make the sound by lightly rubbing their teeth together. It's a very soft sound, but one you'll be happy to hear if it is accompanied by petting or feeding.

Humming. While all rabbits do it on occasion, most rabbit keepers associate it with an unaltered buck wooing his lady love.

Unhappy Rabbit Sounds:

Growling. Rabbits certainly can growl and it often precedes a lunge and possibly a bite. If the rabbit feels threatened (even by you), he'll have no qualms growling and lunging. Forewarned is forearmed.

Snorting. Snorting can come before or along with growling.

Hissing. This sounds exactly the way you think it does. A hiss is used to ward off other rabbits.

Whining or whimpering. Rabbits will whine or whimper if they don't want to be handled. You may hear it particularly from a pregnant doe that has been put into a cage with another rabbit (especially a buck). The whimper is a protest to the environment in which they find themselves. This might include an unwanted cage-mate or in the case of a pregnant doe, a sign that she isn't interested in a buck's advances.

Your Elderly Rabbit

Rabbits in the wild on average live up to 3 years or less. Factors like predation, starvation and exposure to harmful elements, often plays part in shortening the lives of wild rabbits. However, if properly cared for, domestic pet rabbits live on average between 8 and 12 years, depending on the breed. The rabbit with the longest life span on record lived to be 19 years old. Domesticated pet rabbits definitely do live a lot longer life span than their wild cousins. A domesticated rabbit is considered old around 5 - 6 years or more, again, depending on the breed.

The behavior of elderly rabbits can change in a few ways. Older rabbits are usually more sluggish. They will continue the same routines such as litter box practices, but some elderly rabbits may have difficulties stepping into the box. Lowering one of the sides is advisable. Older rabbits tend to sleep more often.

As a rabbit ages, health issues may arise like with any elderly person or animal. Some signs of aging health issues include:

- Skin abscesses
- More frequent intestinal problems
- Kidney and urinary problems
- Dental problems
- Nervous system, eyes and ears problems (runny eye, dacryocystitis for example)
- Heart and respiratory problems
- Obesity (can lead to heart disease, liver disease, digestive problems)
- Cancers
- Decreased ability to fight off infection

Factors that can determine longer life:

- If the rabbit is spayed or neutered hey usually have a longer life span
- Diet
- General care

- Size (Larger the rabbit, the shorter it's average life span will be)
- If the rabbit receives regular vet care or not
- Environment/Housing conditions.
- The genetic makeup of the rabbit.

Routine care for geriatric pets should involve a consistent daily routine and periodic veterinary examinations to assess the presence or progress of chronic disease. Stressful situations and abrupt changes in daily routines should be avoided. If a drastic change must be made to an older pet's routine, try to minimize stress and to implement the change in a gradual manner if possible.

Rabbit Conclusion

We hope you have enjoyed reading "How to Care for Your Rabbit: A Complete Guide from Kitten to Adult" and that you have learned everything you need to know including some extra tips and information to take care of your rabbit. Rabbits make great pets and they can be well behaved and very affectionate and loving companions. We hope your time with your furry friend is a long and happy one and you give it all the love and affection that they deserve and that they will reciprocate this love tenfold.

Thanks for reading "How to Care for Your Rabbit: A Complete Guide from Kit to Adult".
I hope to see you again soon for some more of our popular pet loving books.

If you enjoyed this book or found it useful, please show your support by leaving a review or by clicking on the link below (e-book only):

Thank you for reading

We invite you to share your thoughts and reactions

   Pin It

First Printing, 2017

ISBN: 9781549694899

Top10 Publishing

123 Oval Road

London, NW1 7EA

77563371R00031

Made in the USA
Middletown, DE
22 June 2018